T0148571

MARY ENERGY

ALSO BY THE AUTHORS

The Heart Speaks to The Mind:
Wisdom Stories from the World's Great Masters

Christ: Mother Mary's Gift of Light

Discover Your Divine Destiny and Live with Joy

MARY ENERGY

Mother Mary's Gift of Love

AMARJIT SINGH MODI

ELIZABETH TEMPLE

iUniverse, Inc.
Bloomington

Mary Energy
Mother Mary's Gift of Love

The Scripture quotations contained herein are from the New Revised Standard Version Bible, copyright 1989 by the Division of Christian Education of the National Council of the Churches of Christ in the U.S.A., and are used by permission. All rights reserved.

iUniverse books may be ordered through booksellers or by contacting:

iUniverse
1663 Liberty Drive
Bloomington, IN 47403
www.iuniverse.com
1-800-Authors (1-800-288-4677)

Because of the dynamic nature of the Internet, any web addresses or links contained in this book may have changed since publication and may no longer be valid. The views expressed in this work are solely those of the author and do not necessarily reflect the views of the publisher, and the publisher hereby disclaims any responsibility for them.

Any people depicted in stock imagery provided by Thinkstock are models, and such images are being used for illustrative purposes only.
Certain stock imagery © Thinkstock.

ISBN: 978-1-4620-5720-7 (sc)
ISBN: 978-1-4620-5721-4 (ebk)

Printed in the United States of America

iUniverse rev. date: 10/12/2011

It has been said "God is Love."
Thus, the Heavens seek Love
Earth seeks Love
People seek Love
This is what makes us great.

Haven Travino, The Tao of Healing

CONTENTS

Introduction
ix

Part 1
Mary Energy: The Divine
Mother's Love
1

Part 2
Mary Energy for Parents
17

Part 3
Exercises to Expand Your Love
35

About the Authors
51

❧ INTRODUCTION ❧

Mary Energy is the love that Mary gave to Jesus, filling her child with incomparable bliss. When you connect to Mary Energy you will experience an indescribable joy, beyond all the joys you have ever felt in your lifetime.

When we first began to study Mary, we saw that she played an important role in Jesus' life. She was not an ordinary mother, but a divine being whose gift of love helped her son become a great leader of love. This led us to write *Christ: Mother Mary's Gift of Light*. The more we learned about Mary, the more we appreciated her contribution to the world. We saw that Mary is more than a figure of the past, she is the living energy of love itself. She shared an abundance of love with Jesus, and her love flowed effortlessly from her like light flows from the sun. This is when we began to study the practice of Mary's love. It was no longer enough to admire Mary; we wanted to feel the love she felt. We asked Mary to let us feel her love, and we began to experience Mary Energy in our lives.

All of us have the divine ability to love inherent within us. We only require the inspiration of a great loving being like Mary to remind us of our ability to love and to inspire us to share that love. We can give a great gift of love to those things that are close to our hearts, whether it is our children, parents, pets, or a noble cause. If we experience the joy that Mary felt when she held Jesus in her arms, we can learn to love like Mary, and love everything we come into contact with in a complete, effortless way. We wrote this book to share what we have discovered thus far. Our path is one of total dedication to experience the joy that an expression of true love brings. The gift of Mary Energy is a gift of everlasting joy, first to yourself, then to those you touch, then to the entire world.

In Part 1, we describe what we have learned about Mary's love. In Part 2, some of my great friends share their experiences with Mary Energy in their lives as loving parents. In Part 3, we give exercises to help us increase our connection to Mary Energy. These are the insights of a pioneer group of Mary Energy practitioners. We also welcome new ideas and new understanding of Mary's love. Please add your own wisdom to ours and share what you have learned. Sincere thanks to Kirsten and Matt Biondi, Julie Salisbury, Gayle Gray, Dolores Spivack, Megan MacArthur, Tim Perry, and Harpreet Jeewan for sharing how they have grown in love with their children. Together we offer our deepest gratitude to Mother Mary, for guiding us on the path of love.

Mary connected us to the ultimate experience of joy, and we invite you to experience for yourself this joy beyond which there is no other joy. This book is a gift to you so that you can live with joy forever. Let Mary be with you!

PART 1

Mary Energy: The Divine Mother's Love

Mother of Jesus, Ocean of Love

Mary the mother of Jesus needs no introduction. Every day, billions of Christians around the world feel Mary's presence in their lives. They honor Mary and receive inspiration from the love she gave her son. We studied Mary and immediately felt the effect of her love, too. We saw that Mary gave a gift to the entire universe through her love for her son. We began to regard Mary with incredible reverence and a new level of devotion. We became students of mother Mary, and discovered that her love is an unending source of inspiration to love as she did.

Parents benefit greatly from learning to experience and express Mary's love. Just as a plant cannot grow without water, children cannot grow without love. Children need their parents to be more than caretakers providing basic needs. Children need their parents to fill them with love and inspire them to live with love. And not just ordinary human love, but divine love—the limitless love that fills the universe! Not only can you have a strong, intimate bond with your child, you can also bring great joy to your own life, and to everyone who comes into your life.

We invite you to join us in the practice of Mary's love. When you feel her love you will feel unbelievable warmth radiating from your heart, flowing into all that you do. Learning to love like Mary is learning to shine like the sun. First you will feel the warmth of your love, then those closest to you will feel it, and then you will touch everyone around you. We are in the river, flowing toward the ocean of love. It is a beautiful journey!

Mary's Life with Jesus

As a young woman Mary was visited by an angel named Gabriel. The angel told Mary she would give birth to a son named Jesus, a special child who would become a great leader. The angel Gabriel acknowledged that Mary had a divine capacity to love. He recognized, as we do today, that the mother of the messiah could not be an ordinary woman. God gave Jesus to Mary because Mary had an extraordinary gift to give Jesus, the gift that made it possible for Jesus to fulfill his life's mission. Mary's gift was her extraordinary love.

We can know Mary's gifts to Jesus from the gifts that Jesus gave to the world. Each of us is born with the divine spark of our mission within us, and when our gifts take root in the world, we inspire others and win their support. As an adult, Jesus had so much love that he was able to share it with the entire world, so we know that as a child he must have been loved to an incredible degree. This was Mary's divine purpose, to love Jesus in the special way only she could.

Mary's relationship with Jesus began the moment she knew he would be born to her. From that day forward Mary began to raise her son to become the messiah he was meant to be. She began to create his body from her body, and she began to educate Jesus in the womb. Mary's state of mind educated Jesus' state of mind; Mary's spirit spoke to Jesus' spirit. Mary communicated with Jesus though the energy of love flowing through her body. This was not ordinary human love. This was a much higher love, a jubilant, expansive, spiritual love. Mary fed Jesus with her joy, and surrounded him with God-like love for all creation.

Then imagine how Mary celebrated when Jesus was finally born! How fortunate Jesus was, to be born to parents who anticipated him so eagerly! Born a mother who desired him and knew his great worth! Born to parents who understood their holy relationship to each other! Imagine how Mary beheld newborn Jesus' face, imagine how her heart filled with warmth to see her creation! Then imagine how Mary and Joseph made a joyful home for Jesus. Mary cared for her baby with great tenderness, watching to discern his needs and tending to them with pleasure. Mary and Joseph protected Jesus from harm and went to great lengths to keep him safe. Caring for Jesus gave them immense satisfaction, because every time Mary and Joseph looked at their baby, they remembered their divine purpose on this earth—to share love with Jesus and with each other.

As Jesus grew, Mary was his guide and his teacher. Long before Jesus learned to speak, Mary and Jesus communicated with each other in a language of love and care. Mary held Jesus and pure joy flowed from her body into his.

Mary spoke to Jesus with smiles, with laughter, and with the loving energy in her voice. When Mary played with Jesus she became like a child herself, experiencing the joy of play along with him. She guided Jesus to explore their surroundings, helping him to experience all the sights and sounds of their world. They built a strong bond of trust between them. Mary spoke to Jesus from her heart, she sang songs to him, and she held him and rocked him and kissed him with tremendous affection.

Mary continued to guide Jesus as he grew. She encouraged him to speak with her, she listened to him, and she helped him. She answered Jesus' questions about the world. When Mary didn't know the answer to Jesus' question, she consulted a rabbi to find the answer for him. Mary was his protector and his champion. She watched with pride as Jesus discovered his talents. She felt happiness with him, felt sadness with him, felt wonder and all the broad spectrum of emotions life evokes in us. She observed who her child was as a unique person, and sought to understand and support him.

Mary's example of love taught Jesus to love. When Jesus looked at his mother, he saw that love "bears all things, believes all things, hopes all things, endures all things." He saw that "Love never ends (1 Corinthians 13:7-8)." Mary shared love with Jesus in many, many forms. She gave him joy when she fed his curiosity, when she sang songs and spoke prayers with him. She gave him joy in encouraging words. She gave him joyful experiences in the form of friendships, play and stories, beautiful sights and insights, in all the gifts of life. Jesus felt joy in Mary's presence, and he knew that she supported him.

4

Making Mary Our Teacher

Mary filled her son with such a magnitude and depth of love that he grew up to love all people, and to share an enduring message of love felt by billions of people today. Mary's gift of love was the highest service to God that a parent could possibly give. Mary raised Jesus to become the messiah he was created to be, and she did this with no unusual tools apart from the unusual level of her love. Jesus is quoted as saying, "For each tree is known by its own fruit. Figs are not gathered from thorns, nor are grapes picked from a bramble bush (Luke 6:44)." Mary was the tree and Jesus was the fruit. To raise a son so loving as Jesus, Mary must have been the most loving person who has ever lived!

I call divine love "Mary Energy" The purpose of writing this book and offering it to others is to make Mary our teacher in the practice of Mary Energy. We can learn so much about love from Mary's example. If parents today learn to love their children in the extraordinary way Mary loved Jesus, their children will become gifts to the entire universe. We must go to the next stage of love, and then to the next, and the next. We must learn to feel more joy! We must strengthen and expand our connection to divine love. Any person can do this, simply by remembering Mary's gift to Jesus, feeling the power of her love, and sharing their newly expanded love with others.

You do not have to practice a religion to learn how to love from Mary. Divine love is a universal experience; it is independent of religion and culture. An atheist feels love, a Sufi dancer feels love, a monk feels love, and an African bushman feels love. Every person feels love. Mary is loved by people from cultures around the world, because all people recognize the incredible power of a loving mother. You do not need to be Christian or Jewish, or belong to any religion to practice Mary Energy. Remember, Mary transcends all religions; she is a source of unlimited love.

Learn to Love Your Child the Way Mary Loved Jesus

Mary's example shows that mothers have a powerful ability to bring light to the world by giving the gift of their highest love to their children. A mother's role is much more than the role of nurse or caretaker. A child is not a sheep! Children need more than food and vitamins, a place to sleep and a good school. They need to learn much more, they need to learn to live with love. They need your personal guidance, your faith and your understanding, and they need you to inspire them to feel joy in this lifetime. This is what many children are missing: a close, spiritual relationship with the one who created them.

All parents can fill their children with love, and inspire their children to love. Children are born ready to give you love, and ready to receive all the love you can give them. A mother who shares divine love with her child also receives an incredible benefit. The child will immediately return the mother's love back to her, filling her with joy and inspiring her to love even more. In this way, parents and children can take each other to ever greater levels of love. There is no limit to how high the sharing of love can take us!

Many people first experience "true love" when they hold their child in their arms for the first time. When a mother or father holds their infant, they connect to God-like ability to love. Try to imagine how Mary felt when she first held Jesus. She held a messiah, her creation, in her arms! Even if you do not have a child, you can use this image to connect to Mary Energy. Try to imagine what Mary felt when she looked into Jesus' eyes. Try to see what Jesus saw in Mary's eyes. Try to picture their joy, their amazement, the flood of love, the devotion, the expansion of their hearts and minds! Holding her son, Mary knew her purpose on this earth was much larger than her human body and her human lifetime. She connected to her divine, eternal nature in her love for Jesus. Together Mary and Jesus took on a mission to fulfill the highest destiny, the destiny to love all creation, to love without limit.

When Mary expressed her love to her son, she became connected to the divine source of all love, and her love grew. So Jesus inspired Mary to love, and Mary's love inspired Jesus. Like the reflection of a candle's flame passed between two mirrors, their light continued to multiply. Together they rose to an unparalleled level of love. This love was so high that we feel it today without ever having met them. Every person in the world has the potential for the flame of divine love to burn inside them. Likewise, every person has the ability to express that love with others. We only need the inspiration of a great figure like Mary to ignite the candle within, and the practice sharing our love with our children.

Love Brings Joy

> *"If I speak in the tongues of men and of angels,*
> *but have not love, I am only a resounding*
> *gong or a clanging cymbal. If I have the gift of*
> *prophecy and can fathom all mysteries and all*
> *knowledge, and if I have a faith that can move*

> *mountains, but have not love, I am nothing.*
> *If I give all I possess to the poor and surrender*
> *my body to the flames, but have not love, I gain*
> *nothing (1 Corinthians 13:1-8a)."*

So what is this divine love we keep talking about? **Love is nothing more or less than the experience of pure joy.**

There are many other things parents provide their children, such as food and shelter, help with homework, transportation, money, advice, hugs, presents on their birthday, etc. But none of these things are love. Love is nothing more or less than the experience of pure joy. Sometimes we mistake something for love which isn't. For instance, a parent can feel concern for their child, care very much for the child and want to solve the child's problems, but concern is not joy. So it is possible, in any type of relationship, to feel interest in the other person, and attachment to them, and empathy for their experiences, and responsibility towards them, but still have missed out on the sweetness of love, on tasting joy together!

Joy is found in the heart. We cannot find joy in the mind because joy is not a concept. The mind is for concepts, thoughts and ideas. The heart is for joy. Joy is an experience of the heart filling with love and pouring over. Joy is a wonderful feeling in the body, a feeling of expansion beyond the body. This experience is completely real. You don't need our description because you have experienced it before! Here is a very powerful exercise: Take five minutes to think back on a time in your life when you felt incredible inner joy. It could be one of your highest memories from childhood, or one of your greatest personal moments since. Play the memory like a video in your imagination and re-experience the joy you felt. Feel how you felt then, that expansive feeling in your heart, and just joy and joy and joy. When you are finished, tell yourself aloud, "This is who I am." It's true! Love is your true nature. The only reason you are here on this planet is to experience joy and to share it with others.

Ignite the Candle of Love Within You

Remembering who you truly are is the first step in practicing Mary Energy. The great psychologist Carl Jung said, "I am who I was." He remembered, or realized, that he was presently the spark of the eternal divine that he was before he was born. You were born from the eternal, and you hold within you still the spark of the divine you were before your birth. When the angel Gabriel appeared to Mary, she remembered her true nature as a divine being, a person with a unique purpose in human history, a living expression of God's love. She must have known this as her true identity, for she accepted the mission to raise God's child on earth. Think about Mary's embodiment of the eternal, and think about the divine spark of the eternal within yourself.

To help us connect to our original nature, we can imagine one thousand ways that Mary experienced joy with Jesus. For instance, picture the following scene: when Jesus was a baby, Mary first made him calm and comfortable, and then she held him facing her on her lap. Jesus could not even speak yet, so they just gazed at each other in amazement. Mary and Jesus looked into each other's eyes. Then one of them saw the light, or joy, in the other's eyes and began to smile, just a very small smile. The other one saw this smile and it made them feel a bit more joy, and began to smile, increasing the other's feeling of joy. The joy built each time it passed from Mary to Jesus and from Jesus to Mary, until they both burst out laughing! This is what happens between a loving mother and infant, and most of us have had this experience with someone we love. So remembering our loving nature does not require complicated techniques, and sometimes not even words. It costs no money and requires no special schooling. Mother Mary went higher than any human has, without a car, a phone, a bank account, or much of anything else we consider necessary.

You were born from love, you were born with love, and you are born to love. So practicing Mary's love is not difficult. Igniting the love within means returning to your home, like returning a fish to water. If you become temporarily disconnected from your divine nature, Mary can reconnect you. If you forget who you are, Mary can remind you. Even if you do not feel one drop of love within, your love is still there! You only need the influence of a great loving being to ignite your love. Mary can be that influence, like a match lighting a candle, and then you will know your love is always there. We can get our ignition from a great loving being like Mary, from loving a young child, or even a loved animal or even a plant.

The Experience of Mary Energy

The second part of practicing Mary Energy is simply experiencing it! The energy of limitless love is not a philosophical concept. It is a natural force like electricity. You will know that Mary Energy is real when you experience it for yourself. If you touch fire and it burns you, you trust that the fire is real fire, because it has done what fire does. You would never say it was fire if you touched the flame and it did not burn you, for it did not have the effect of fire. The same is true of divine love. If you pray to Mary and feel nothing, that is not Mary Energy. When you feel immense joy, you know what it is without a doubt, and it does not matter the name we give it. Practicing Mary Energy means using the inspiring figure of mother Mary to connect to an inner experience of joy—this inner joy is the human birthright.

Honestly, the experience of Mary Energy cannot be described. Such joy renders you speechless! Even afterward, there are no words to describe it. Even the great poet Lao Tze, when he experienced the universe unfolding before him, all he could say was ",I'm amazed, and amazed, and amazed . . ." Imagine describing the taste of mango to a child who has never eaten it. You could say, "Mango is sweet," but no description would give the taste of mango to the child. We understand this, so when we want a child to experience something wonderful, we give it to them to experience for themselves. The only way to understand the taste of mango is to taste it, and it is the same with Mary Energy. We must experience it to know what it is, and we may attempt to describe it, but no words can give the experience.

It is your nature to love just as it is the sun's nature to give light and heat. The sun does not make a special effort to burn! The sun merely expresses its nature. The same is true for you. Love is your nature, and joy is your very essence. Your true nature is an effortless expression of love, constant and independent of external circumstances. Likewise, your connection to divine love is impossible to sever. If a storm comes, we may not be able to see the sun for a time, but the worst storm in life can do nothing to your essential loving nature. Also, do you think the sun ever feels cold? Of course not! And the person who connects to their inner joy cannot feel anything but joy—they are the first to benefit from the heat and light of their love.

Love Grows Through Sharing

The final step in Mary Energy practice is to share your love. We must share Mary Energy in our daily lives. When we share, the love grows, and then we have more love to share. If you do not share, you remain limited to what you already know and cannot grow. This is why all the great teachers of the world—whether they are healers, musicians, writers, spiritual people—they share everything they know. They hold nothing back, because they know that by sharing they learn, and therefore have more to share. As in Saint Francis' prayer, *"Grant that I may not so much seek . . . to be loved, as to love. For it is in giving that we receive . . . "*

Sharing is not difficult. It does not mean talking about Mary Energy. Sharing means expressing your love, and it happens naturally. When you feel an abundance of love inside yourself, the love overflows and spills out into whatever you are doing. When you feel joy, others also feel joy. They are reminded of their own true nature, of their own higher ability to love.

When you feel joy you want to express it in the world. It can be feeling joy with any person, with your cat, with nature, or with your voice in song. Joy must be shared in order to grow; love must be expressed in order for it to live. The seed kept in the pocket remains a single seed, but the planed seen can multiply one hundred times, or more! How do we know when we are expressing our love? We know when we see joy around us. The result of expressing love is bringing joy to the earth.

We can express Mary Energy with any person, or alone, at any time. Sharing Mary Energy with a young child is especially rewarding because children readily accept your love. Children reflect the love they receive the way the moon reflects the sun's light. The child returns the love to the parent, and this only inspires the parent to love more. This was the relationship between Mary and Jesus. Each one's love raised the other to a higher level. There is no limit to how high this reflection of love can take us!

Sharing Mary Energy will change your life:
Through sharing your love with your unborn baby, the baby will be born happy, with no conflicts.
Through sharing your love with your child, you will support the child to discover and fulfill their divine destiny.
Through sharing your love you will transform yourself and fulfill your own divine destiny.
Through sharing your love with others, you will give your highest gift to life, filling your life with meaning and purpose.

Mary Energy and Unconditional Love

Mary Energy includes the concept of unconditional love, however, Mary Energy goes far beyond unconditional love. Practicing unconditional love means breaking down barriers in the mind so that love may flow. Each person has different barriers blocking their ability to express love, and each person has different experiences of removing those conditions to love more freely. This is learning to love without qualifications or conditions.
In contrast, Mary Energy is an entirely new level of love. It is the unparalleled expression of divine love that Mary gave to Jesus. It is as powerful as the boundless energy of the cosmos,

a level of love we cannot conceive of with our limited minds! Practicing Mary Energy is attempting to approach the level of Mary's experience of divine love. We may be able to feel 50% or 60% of what Mary shared with Jesus, and that amount would be the peak experience of a lifetime!

Mary Energy is much more than love without conditions. It is the immeasurable joy that flowed from Mary's heart into Jesus and throughout the world. It is so powerful that we feel it today even though few have expressed it in the two thousand years since! Mary Energy is love that inspires one to love. It is love that reveals that there is *no upper limit* to love. Mary Energy is a **mission**.

Mary the Messiah

The biblical prophecy of lineage stated that the Jewish messiah would come from the tribe of David. When Mary was born they did not accept her as the messiah because she was female. Her gifts were her gifts, but they were not ready to recognize them. When Mary's child was male, they accepted him as the fulfillment of the prophecy. Today we cannot say that Mary wasn't a messiah because she was female. It is the energy she carried that makes her a messiah, not the physical body or the clothes she wears! None of us are an ocean of love like Mary, and none of us love as she did. We celebrate Mary as the messiah of love.

Mary was an unusual being with an incredible love. She was aware of her holy role in her child's life from the very beginning. She raised him with the highest love imaginable, and with her boundless love he was able to grow up to fulfill his holy purpose. In the act of loving her son so fully, Mary made an everlasting gift to the world, and this is why we love her still today. Mary gave us many wonderful insights:

Mary's example shows the profound opportunity that parents have to inspire their children to love.
Mary's example shows the incredibly far-reaching power of divine love on future generations.
Mary's example shows that love is the key to fulfillment of one's life purpose.
Mary's example shows the potential for a divine relationship between a mother and child, even before birth.
Mary's example shows that a woman can be a great prophet.
Mary's example shows that any regular person can go very high in this lifetime simply by sharing the love inside them.

Now the world is ready to accept Mary as a messiah. We are experiencing a global shift of energy from the competitive to the cooperative, toward love. This is a shift toward feminine energy, toward the power of the loving mother. "Mary Energy" is the energy of limitless love. It is a name for the divine love which is available to every person on earth. In this all-encompassing love there is no pain, no fear, and no sadness. To become Mary's student is to remember our power to love regardless of the circumstances. We can use Mary as a guide, as a connection to the spirit of boundless love, and as an example of the God-like love we all possess. Mary can remind us of our divine gift of love, and teach us to express this love wherever we go.

From Worship to Action

After two thousand years of showing Mary honor, devotion and love, we have made her our friend. The next stage now is to learn from her and practice her love. The real benefit is not to talk about her love, but to experience it for ourselves! Now is the time to bring the concept of the highest form of love into our daily lives, into expression and action. Mary Energy has a great ability to heal, to nurture, and to celebrate. Practicing Mary Energy hurts no one, it simply brings joy to the earth.

Prophets periodically come to earth to remind us of our divine nature. These advanced spirits live as humans to show us the heights we are capable of in our own lives. Prophets do not come to say, "Worship me," they come to say, "Do what I do! Follow my example and reap the rewards!" No good teacher says, "You cannot do what I have done." In fact, all great teachers want their students to become like them, to do what they do, and to surpass them. They share their wisdom so that the people who admire them can learn their practices and begin to live as they live.

Mary is a wonderful, generous teacher. The entire world is amazed by her love. She came to remind us who we truly are, loving beings capable of truly astonishing expressions of love. The highest way to honor Mary's contribution is to make her our teacher in the practice of divine love, and learn to love our children the way she loved Jesus. If we love the way Mary loved Jesus, we have moved beyond worship into action, and no prayer can honor her more! Every human is capable of a love as great as Mary's. She used normal human capabilities, she only expressed her divine power to love. You, too, are capable of incredible love. Her love lives within you!

PART 2

Mary Energy for Parents

Overwhelming Love
by Kirsten & Matt Biondi

When I hold my daughter, I feel warmth and love streaming through my body. I love to look into her eyes when she is nursing and connect with this child. I knew there was one more baby that was going to come through my body. For years I felt as if our family was riding in a car, and there was something—something like a balloon on a long string—flapping out the window as we went along. I kept looking, checking, the noise was a distraction. I know, I know, I would say to this person. I would say, I get it . . . go talk to your dad.

Once she was born, I would hold her and always have this overwhelming feeling of gratitude. I would whisper in her ear, "Thank you for coming to our family." Even now, I tell her that when we embrace. I finally feel like our family is complete, that our family, in our "car," is all intact—the window is up and we are moving forward. I no longer feel like I'm leaving someone behind.

I feel so grateful to have this feeling fulfilled, and it brings me so much joy and deep satisfaction to pour love into her and watch her blossom. I don't know what she will do with her own life, but it is interesting to notice the things she is drawn to and where her natural tendencies take her.

To Mother Like Many, or Like Mary?
by Julie Salisbury

*"When I find myself in times of trouble,
Mother Mary comes to me, speaking words of
wisdom, let it be."*
The Beatles, "Let It Be"

Oh yes, please, let it be. Let it be true that there is someone out there speaking to us with gentle words of wisdom during our times of trouble. And as a mother, those times of trouble can arise quickly and at unexpected intervals. Even among the best of us, our fears, worries and self-doubts intersperse with our judgments, insecurities and emotional wounds to create a mixed-up mélange of uncertain and inconsistent action.

Still, we devour the latest parenting books, spend hours searching the web (often to our horror) and ask trusted friends countless questions, but there are some times when nothing short of divine intervention—Mother Mary?—can save us from ourselves.

Many answers to our own parenting questions can be found in the way that Mary loved Jesus. And as we try to listen to the words of wisdom she embodied in her own mothering, we find it's not an easy path. It's one that is fraught with risk, pain, loss and fear. Mary knew from the moment of conception that her child would suffer. Who of us would want that? But hers is also a path of great joy—expressed most beautifully in *The Magnificat*. And as she welcomes her responsibility to love unconditionally, she gives the world a Child who is free to fully pursue His own divine destiny. And as she loves Him, His own ability to love becomes magnified.

How many of us could do what Mary did as a mother? Think back to that first moment when an angel appears to Mary, giving her the news that she is carrying the Messiah. He tells her, "Be not afraid." Are you kidding me? I was frightened to death during my entire first pregnancy, and I was 36 years old, married, in a financially stable country with outstanding medical care. I would have been petrified as a young, inexperienced peasant girl, seeing an apparition and given news containing equal parts responsibility and implausibility. I would have dropped to my knees and begged to be released from this madness. No thanks, not me. Pick someone else for that job please.

But Mary accepts and believes. Her faith tells her that she has been chosen for this task. That it is her destiny. That she is an important part of the story. That all she has to do is love. What if we really accepted and believed that about our own parenting?

As simple as that sounds, it isn't easy in our society. Our world is highly competitive. We camp out for slots in the "best" preschool, fearing that if our child doesn't get in, we've sabotaged their chances for a top tier college. We over-schedule our children with sports, art, performances, foreign language and the finest tutors, all in an effort to "produce" the well-rounded child. We're surrounded by people who judge us and our children by our shortcomings, or who are too insecure themselves to acknowledge the innate strengths in our differences.

But what if we believed that all children are perfectly made? And that we, too, are perfectly made in the divine image of God. How would that change our parenting? How would that deepen our ability to love, and magnify the love our child can bring to the world?

All humans face challenges. That means we and our children will too. We hope the challenges won't be Christ-like in their proportions, and as we love our children we work so hard to protect them from suffering, pain and challenges. But sometimes that sense of protection can steer us into the murky waters of wanting a "perfect" child.

My first experience with motherhood was actually as a step-mom to a model child. I had the good fortune to truly love his father, and to care for and respect his "true" mom as well. This child was and is remarkable. He is highly intelligent, but deeply sensitive. Always mature for his age, with a quick wit and an endearingly silly streak. A great athlete with stellar test scores who looks just like his Dad. I found myself asking, "What more could I want in a child, and how quickly can I have some of my own? Just like this one, please."

My own first son was born full of energy and with an insatiable zest for life. That's a nice way of saying, "He was a handful." My husband used to look at me with a shrug of exhaustion and say, "Well, you can't teach zeal," and this child was clearly born with enough for a roomful of TV pitchmen. He ran non-stop beginning at 10 months, never slept and didn't talk until he was well past two. He suffered what may have been a mild seizure at age three, and developed chronic migraine headaches that caused him to virtually pass out.

It was nearly impossible for me to avoid comparing him with other children, especially his older half-brother, who was always calm, polite, highly articulate, healthy, and exceptionally mature. So we took my young son to every specialist we could find—pediatricians, neurologists, speech and occupational therapy professionals. Nothing was wrong, but something wasn't right.

But whenever I was with this child, I felt a special lightness of being. His own happiness, and yes even his zeal, was infectious. There were so many times when I felt almost overwhelmed by my love for him, but one night in particular comes to mind. We were at the beach, and it was a typical sleepless night. I was up for the fourth or fifth time with him, and finally gave in to holding him and rocking him to sleep. As he calmed in my arms and peered at me with his sweet, glowing face, I felt bathed in light and love—like I was being baptized. I knew in that moment that my child was a miracle—that all children are miracles—just as they are.

Maybe it was the sleep deprivation, but I think it was a gift of Mary Energy. As I continued to love this child, dropping the specialists and letting him be who he was meant to be, he began to truly blossom. Today he is very different from his older brother, but exactly who I would want him to be in every possible way. He is exceptionally kind, thoughtful and considerate. He is highly creative and a phenomenally abstract thinker. And perhaps because of his zest for life, he wants others around him to enjoy things as much as he does. It makes for a winning combination.

My daughter was born six weeks early via emergency c-section, after placenta abruptia. I lost so much blood that the doctors told us it had been a close call for both of us. Mercifully, my baby girl was remarkably healthy, active and animated. However, I worried and fretted over her every hiccup and was afraid to leave her alone for months. But at every turn, it seemed she was showing me exactly how strong she really was. She refused the bottle, no matter how hungry she may be, and ended up going straight from the breast to drinking from a cup.

This girl demonstrated her independence, her strong will and individualism from the incubator forward. At fourteen months, she would refuse to go downstairs before selecting the perfect pair of shoes to go with her pajamas. This often took quite some time and of course never resulted in bedroom slippers. Over time, I remembered the moment of Mary Energy in the rocking chair and began to see and appreciate my daughter for who she was truly made to be, rather than engage in battle over the trivial.

Today I tell people that she is the most creative person I've ever met. And for a mom who made her career in advertising, marketing and public relations, that's saying quite a bit. My daughter is powerful, confident and unyielding—and I am in her corner, even when she's disagreeing with me. That's who she is, who she was meant to be, and I love her even more for it.

There's good reason that John 3:16 is the most often quoted of the Scriptures. *"For God so loved the world that He gave His one and only Son, that whosoever believes in Him shall not perish, but have everlasting life."* God loved the world so much, that He gave us His Son to offer redemption from our human frailties. But Mary loved Jesus so much, that she let Him be Jesus. And in so doing, she taught Him to love even more deeply.

As I write this now, thinking back on my life so far as a mother, I feel another moment of Mary wisdom as I remember the tomb of Jesus. After witnessing His arrest, His horrific torture, and His grueling crucifixion, it was Mary (both Mary's actually) who was there at the tomb when the stone was rolled away. Because of her faith, her patience, her perseverance and her love, she was the first to witness the news of the Resurrection—again directly from an angel.

Clearly, we are all not Mary and we don't hear from angels. At least not regularly. But when we allow ourselves to love our children unconditionally, to see the unique miracles they bring to us by being exactly who they are and were meant to be, then in that way we, too, witness a resurrection. We allow our children the new life that comes with living their divine destiny. And what a journey that can be. Let it be. Yes please, let it be.

> *"Before every human being comes*
> *a retinue of angels, announcing, make way*
> *for an image of the Holy one.*
> *Blessed be He."*
> Hasidic Teaching

A Love Letter to My Baby Boy
by Gayle Gray, mother of Damon Furberg

One day long ago, I awakened to the sound of a hummingbird beating its frantic wings against the window above my bed. By the time I realized the source of that desperate fluttering, my precious little friend was lying unconscious on the sill. I picked up his inert body, and stroking it gently, moved toward the balcony door. Stepping onto the deck, I looked beyond the railing to the bright blue sky, the restful pond below, and the sleepy field that was peacefully climbing up the gradual inclination of the hillside. This was the world my friend inhabited. For him, what a strange and frightening place was the inside of a human habitat, with unyielding windows, and hard impenetrable walls.

My heart was breaking for the hummingbird's misfortune, yet the feel of his soft warm body folded into my hand, filled me with an indescribably delicious and unconditional love. I stood there for a few moments enjoying the texture of his soft silky wings, and the loveliness of his iridescent ruby throat, marveling at the tenacity and valor of such an utterly vulnerable being. Suddenly I felt a stirring, a slight twitching; and before I realized what was happening, he flew into the air without a backward glance. As he wended his way back to the familiarity of his world, a perfect sweetness settled over me. I had touched a spark of God, and all was right and good, even if just for that one moment.

Telling you the hummingbird story is my way of expressing the wonder of your existence. Miraculously, out of the vast expanse of the cosmos, energy and matter converge to create a gift glorious and sublime—a precious newborn baby, with hair as soft as bird feathers, skin like the morning dew, and a fragile little body that has leapt courageously from non-being into being. Cradling you in my arms, I feel the warmth and solidity of your compact little body, and watch the rise and fall of your chest, your breathing full of danger and possibility. Breathing in, the world enters, breathing out, time stops. I watch like a mother tiger, ready to pounce and destroy, no intrusion too insignificant to go unnoticed. You are the reason I live, the purpose for which my body has been crafted into womanhood. No experience earthly or divine will ever come close in beauty, love and intensity to the moment when I first laid eyes on you. Thank you precious hummingbird, for bringing such mystery and sweetness to my world.

> *"That which sings and contemplates in you,*
> *Is still dwelling within the bounds*
> *Of that first moment which scattered*
> *The stars into space."*
> Kahlil Gibran

Motherhood: Chaos followed by Listening then Love
by Dolores Spivack

My three children are now 21, 19 and 17 years old. This is the story of our journey during the formative years of their lives, ages one through four. Throughout the years that my husband and I have raised them, CHAOS, LISTENING, then LOVE—in various degrees—have marked the growth for all the members in our nuclear family. We all have worked and continue to work hard to achieve this. Let me tell you how.

Chaos

There are many paths to the same goal of mothering. Any mother strives for healthy and reasonably balanced children who are ready to take their place in society as contributing members. Parenting paths—like paths in the forest—can change, meander, diverge, slow down even to a stop, and race forward depending on circumstances and resources. Often, chaos came to visit our home as an unwelcomed guest. These were the moments of my greatest doubts as a nurturer to my children. Only when I embraced chaos as a temporary guest did we learn lessons from chaos. The negative "chaos" became a positive "circus." The problem of chaos became a solution from which to learn. Chaos always left but I knew it would return again at different times and circumstances. When chaos returned I chose not to doubt my abilities, only to continue to love my children no matter what!

Listening

Babies don't come with instruction manuals. But the road map for their development is easy: just listen to their energies. Their energies will guide the mother to help guide the child. At certain times, energies are slow and should be sustained or re-energized. At other times, children's energies are over-activated and should be calmed. But at all times children's energies should be comforted and directed toward positive endeavors. I listened to the energies of my children. Born into the same environment, same parents, all three children had different types of energies. These energies must be noticed, directed and encouraged. One child loved tinkering with things: stacking blocks, banging pots and pans to hear different sounds, assembling books, etc. I gave him things to stack and bang. He is studying engineering today. My middle child loved to watch people and draw shapes. Who knew she was looking at the shape of people's mouths? Today she hopes to become a dentist. My youngest loved to count and compare things: this pile of cans is bigger than that pile of cans. I gave him more cans. He hopes to become a statistician. I listened to the different energies of my children and this worked to the benefit of all. By listening to my children it became crystal clear what each of them needed. They in as much clearly told me what they wanted even before they could speak. All I had to do was listen to them.

Love

There is only one rule of thumb: just love your children no matter what, no matter where, no matter how. Unconditional love fosters unconditional joy for all. Since all of my children were close in age, whirlwind activities and sometimes whirlwind anxieties were the everyday experience. There are many moments of my past that are a blur and grabbing joy was a challenge. I kept reminding myself that I must enjoy the moment. It's the journey not the destination which is most important. This blur will not last forever, so enjoy the temporary insanity. Many times I felt my youngest child did not receive enough of my attentions during the busy day. He was and is an easy spirit. But when he was almost eighteen months old often he would wake in the middle of the night when I and everyone were asleep. I'd take him into bed but he did not want to lie quietly. So I would take him on the couch and lay down with him. We did not have to play or even sing or talk, no music, no television. Just hugging as we both fell asleep was enough for both him and me. So our one-on-one quality time was in the middle of the night doing nothing. We both enjoyed this. But this worked because out of this joy came love.

Chaos, listening then love provided an opportunity for me to grow. And chaos, listening and love allowed me to help my children grow. Yes, out of chaos, my children became my best teachers when they taught me to listen and grow in love!

The Divine Gifts of Meira & Portia
by Megan MacArthur

Meira

"I know how you feel." These were the first words to fall upon the ears of my eldest daughter.

After a wild childbirth she was placed upon my chest, my partner in this crazy event. We had an instant soul connection and "holy cow that was crazy" understanding together. Neither of us had been there before—or we had and we were at it again. We were partners/sisters from the beginning. Born to me as Meira MacArthur Bonnici, during pregnancy and from this moment on, we were equal players in our life together. My sister. My daughter.

Meira walks the nature path—the artist's route. She sees the world through color, shape, light and depth. She welcomes images and impressions and recreates them to be miracles on paper, in shape, in space. I see her as the filter for my eyes to bring beauty to everything through her perspective and creations of art. Her pure vision and ability to see without judgment creates pure honest art.

Meira is my art. Her name is a Hebrew name meaning vision or light, and so she is—she is my vision and light in my life. Choosing her name in utero, she had it all planned out. Here she is, the visionary, the seer and worker of light—on me and through her art. She is art as she plays, as she grows, and as she tests the boundaries of the world through her days. She is a creation of past, present and future as she processes the tangible depths of life.

Meira. We are twin flames. She is the eldest, the Leo, the loner and the leader, as was I. She navigates to balance the powerful and the powerless. It is a struggle and a gift to have such strength and such fear. Her art is the escape—the real life—the way to allow this world to be freely existent. For me it is the dance. We move through life together and recognize and care for each other knowing we are safe in our expression and processing of this life—we are in love with life through the eyes of art and beauty—a world of freedom we see in each other the pure essence of who we are.

We are two. We are sisters. Together we will continue to understand the world with deeper love and understanding for this place and the creatures we share this existence with—we are safe in our knowledge of our own expression. I have been given such a gift—Meira—to allow me to recognize this aspect of myself. Meira has taught me how to love my dance, and to feel safe resting in the world dance allows me—the place where everything is beauty, everything is art, everything has a purpose as it is shared from a place of pure artistic expression. It is a place of non-attachment, and from this place I feel safe. From this place Meira and I are safe. We are in bliss through pure expression together.

Portia

"Two weeks late and counting." "Amniocentesis." "She's too small."

All of these comments were brought to me, and many more. It was a pregnancy of weekly monitoring. I danced my way through the nine-plus months—rhythm, music, vibration, sound, silence and laughter filled the air for my second daughter. Drum beats and play surrounded my belly as she grew slowly yet consistently.

Portia. She named herself as we sat one night around the dinner table sharing family stories of names and people in our worlds until Tutu, my grandmother from the other side, named her from Shakespeare. She brought forward the name Portia—the powerful female presence from *The Merchant of Venice*. Portia of peace.

She was Portia of safety and security—needing it, not always feeling it. And she was ready to hang out in utero for a mighty long time until she had to be induced to join us outside. Once the pitocin hit it was 20 minutes and she was in my arms. An angel.

This one was the love baby, the one to be admired, the precious baby. With Portia I spent every moment with her as an infant telling her how beautiful she is, how much I wanted to keep her, how much I love her. Over and over again. "Can I keep her?" was my daily question. In love with this baby, I understood what mothers feel. Unlike the partnership with my eldest, who is my deepest love sister, Portia was my little precious angel—something I would never imagine myself feeling, let alone saying.

Portia of peace—no loud noises, patience is taught, love is shared and conflict is limited. She is mighty in her peace and powerful in her mystical presence. The magical baby. Portia is the mystic dancer, the magician. She spins her web of control around the situation and alchemically changes the moment to joy, to ease, or to love. She brings out the magic in me and in all she meets. Through her fearless love of beauty she leads others to be in the same—the beauty of life.

Her dance is one of celebration. No need to process life, she accepts it and moves on through directly into the celebration of it. Portia guides me beyond my ego and into my potential. She is sensitive to energies all around her and I see my path as one to assist her in shielding and processing such influences to make the space available, always for her to create her magic. Portia keeps me in my body, calls me on my anger or fears, and celebrates with me in my joy.

In turn I celebrate her to the highest degree. Portia is my teacher and my love.

The New Manhood
by Tim Perry

Sebastian was supposed to be a girl. In my mind and heart he was, until Carla got an ultrasound and the evidence of his gender was unmistakable. I was shocked to know I was going to have a son. To be the father to a girl seemed so much easier. I could love a girl but not have to model a man's life. With a girl I could be the loving, fun papa without having to be his perfect example of being a man. I have never considered myself weak, or fearful. I have been on adventures around the world and faced danger many times during those adventures, and in my profession as a helicopter pilot. But I have still never felt connected to what would make me a part of the tribe of men. Because love and gentleness has always been at the foundation of who I am, I have never understood the mind of the warrior, bully or brute. I have always revered intellect over brute force, love over domination, kindness over greed, and because of this men have set me apart from them and my friendships with men have been have been few and fleeting. I have longed my whole life for male friendship, to be part of the tribe, to be welcomed to dance around the fire with the warriors, to have the chance to share stories and experiences with my kind. I have braved mountains, deserts, the depths of the ocean, frozen wastelands and the tempest of the air and heart alone, and have hungered for this connection.

So considering my own tenuous relationship to my maleness, I watched the black-and-white images of my strong beautiful man child as a beam of sound illuminated this fantastic male being entrusted to me to guide into manhood. I would be able to teach him what men traditionally do. I could instill in him a profound sense of adventure, of fearlessness. I could make his body strong, his mind sharp, but how could I teach him to be more manly than me, manly enough to join the tribe of men that had eluded me my entire life? It was only then, seeing him swimming in the warm ocean of his mother's womb that I realized he was already teaching me one of thousands of lessons yet to come. A lesson in self-acceptance. My responsibility as his father was not to teach him to be a man, but a good human being guided through his life by his heart. He could be kind, loving and strong. He could be brave, wise and caring. I understood in those few moments what I had struggled with for forty-four years. I had become a good man, and to do so I had to be apart from the tribe, to learn for him the lessons he would need to be a loving man.

I don't think we knew when we named him that his name would embody everything it would mean to be a part of the new manhood this world needs for a new Earth to flourish. Sebastian, as in St. Sebastian martyred for faith in God, Sage, as in one who embodies wisdom, and Lalamilo, his Hawaiian name. Lalamilo was given to him by a kahuna when burying his umbilical cord under palm on the shore near his birth, connecting forever to Mother Earth. Lala is the strong central branch that gives strength to the Milo tree. The ancient Hawaiians made sacred articles from the Milo because of its beauty and strength.

Sebastian Sage Lalamilo, Faithful in the Divine, Wise, Beautiful, and Strong.

*"Being deeply loved by someone
gives you strength;
Loving someone deeply
gives you courage."*
Lao Tzu

Touch from God
by Harpreet Jeewan

Child is a source of energy. When my one year old son hugs me, I actually feel a flow of energy directly from God. He is my connection with God. His touch gives me peace.

Child and flower are similar. They are tender, colorful, give fragrance, need your care and love to grow. When they grow with your love the fruit is sweet.

It is amazing, one day some issue was hanging my mind since morning. I was upset, I did not want to share with anyone but I wanted a relief from that issue. My one year old son behaved in different way on that day. Out of fifteen people I met on that day no one came to know that I was upset. When I came home, my little son kept on hugging me again and again. His hug was so tight, a child of one year old, gave a message of God through his hug. He was looking at me again and again kissed me so many times and continued repeating it for some time. I felt the love of God and a flow of positive energy in me.

Child is image of God and very close to HIM. My son was just seven or eight days old. I was looking at him and thinking that I would not develop emotional ties with him since I feel so tied up with my elder son, being emotionally attached to him. He immediately held my finger very tightly and started looking towards me. And I was hooked.

❧❧ PART 3 ❧❧

Exercises to Expand Your Love

❧ Exercise 1: Positive Influences for Pregnant Women

A mother's state of mind is the single most important factor in her baby's development. Food and vitamins provide for the structure of the baby's body, but only love brings joy to the child's spirit. The mother's thoughts, her emotions and her mindset, these things shape the person her baby will become. If you bring out your highest love during your pregnancy, your baby will be born without conflicts, ready to celebrate life.

The idea is to examine your environment and your habits, and make any improvements that support your connection to inner joy. Watch the effect your daily life has on your emotions, and make your personal world a place where you can express your love more and more. A mother is an unborn child's entire environment. Make your body a temple of love, and your baby will be born happy and shining!

Women naturally feel this attraction to positive influences when they are pregnant. The concerns of daily life are insignificant in comparison to their new love, and so the old worries and problems fade away in the light of their new purpose. Just imagine Mary receiving the announcement of Jesus' coming from the angel Gabriel. Mary could not be the same person after that day. No, this news changed her life! No one could continue to live the same way after learning they would give birth to a king. From the day she knew Jesus was coming, Mary was drawn to new ideas and different influences. She was highly inspired to give her best to life by making the gift of her son a very, very beautiful gift. Let Mary's example light this same kind of fire of love within you. See yourself like Mary, whose work was far too important to let anything disturb her once-in-history opportunity to love her son.

The following areas can be used to support your ability to express Mary's love:

<u>Food</u>. Eat wholesome and nutritious foods as best you can. Eat slowly and enjoy your food. Mealtime is an excellent time to appreciate your body—your body has the amazing ability to craft another human being without your conscious effort! Follow the wisdom of your body as to when to eat and what to eat. Remember that most people in most times have eaten very simple foods and given birth to healthy babies.

<u>Sleep</u>. Peaceful sleep gives strength to the body and clarity to the mind. Your need for sleep or rest may change when you are pregnant. Set aside enough time to sleep until you feel refreshed, and try to make space in your schedule for naps if you need them. Dreams are another source of information for many women when they are pregnant. Some receive messages from the baby, or see their child fully grown. If you have a question, hold it in your mind as you fall asleep, and you may find the answer in your dreams. Spend some

time contemplating what Mary might have dreamed when she was pregnant with Jesus!

Pleasure. Sensory pleasure also nourishes the body, mind, and spirit. Make some time each day to enjoy the beautiful sights, sounds, and sensations in your environment. By doing so, you are building love of life into your child's heart. Watch a sunrise or sunset, take a leisurely walk in nature, sit by a river or ocean, take a swim, take a massage, enjoy gentle yoga or dance, and so on. Do what makes you happy.

Look up to the sky on a sunny day, close your eyes and enjoy the warmth of the sun on your face—something this simple can reconnect you to Mary Energy in the middle of a busy day. Take any action which makes your heart feel light and free. This energy actually encourages your child to grow. You are telling your baby, "Jump for joy! You are coming to a world filled with beautiful experiences!"

Relaxation and Meditation. It is very beneficial to take time each day to clear your thoughts. You can do this by meditating, taking a walk in nature, quiet breathing or prayer, writing your reflections in a journal, or talking out any worries with someone you trust.

In whichever way you prefer, take a peaceful break from your daily activities and let go of your thoughts and daily concerns. Once your mind is clear, feed your mind a new idea to dwell on. Love is one of the best and highest thoughts. Think of your love for your baby, or Mary's love for Jesus, or your love for your own mother. Or try to fathom the immensity of the love of every mother around the world from the time the first baby was born up to this moment!

For meditation, begin by sitting quietly for 15 minutes each day. Sit comfortably with your eyes softly closed, and watch your thoughts come and go like waves. As your mind grows quiet, enjoy existing in a state of "being." Or try having a meditative conversation with Mary. Close your eyes and imagine that you are sitting with Mary in her house in Nazareth, playing on the floor with young Jesus. Continue until you feel that you are really sitting together like good friends. Then ask Mary your questions about motherhood, tell her your concerns about raising your child. Then listen to what Mary tells you. You may be surprised by the answers you receive!

<u>Music</u>. Music has an especially powerful effect on thoughts and mood. Listen to music that lifts your spirit. Your child feels your joy and celebrates with you. Sing, play an instrument, or do some free movement or dance to increase your joy.

<u>Reading and Media</u>. As with music, what we read leads our energies in that direction. You may be drawn to learn about new subjects or discover new interests.

If you read books regarding pregnancy, childbirth, and the care of children, read what inspires and supports your own inner wisdom. Avoid any materials that predict difficulties or undermine your confidence in your abilities. The best knowledge of your body comes from you.

<u>Advice</u>. Also watch the well-meaning advice of your friends and family. You are not obligated to take anyone's suggestions. Every person has a different idea of what is right to do. Take the advice that benefits you, and don't listen if anyone tries to frighten or shame you. Listen to your own instincts regarding your life and the care of your body and your baby.

<u>Positive Voices</u>. Children in the womb can clearly hear the sounds around them. Spend time with people that you want your child to know when s/he is born, and the baby will become familiar with their voices even before they meet! Avoid harsh or negative environments and walk away from arguments. The most important voice your baby hears is your own. It is very powerful for your baby to hear their mother's voice filled with positive emotion.

Spend time with friends that make you laugh. Spend time with people who fill you with joy when you see them. If no one is available, watch movies that make you laugh or read books about beautiful and inspiring subjects. There is no better vitamin for your child than your own joy.

Exercise 2: Educate Your Baby in the Womb

A baby learns from its mother even before birth. Everything you do when you are pregnant you do together with your baby. All of the thoughts and feelings of the mother are shared with her baby. The baby benefits from the best feelings and highest thoughts flowing through your body. In order to educate your baby, watch your thoughts and your feelings throughout the day and monitor them the way you would if you were speaking aloud to your child.

Your child will help you do this. In choosing you (out of all the women in the world!) to bring him or her to life, your baby makes you remember your God-like power of creation. Your child monitors your well-being, and reminds you that you are a powerful creator. You remember that you have a much larger work at hand, and you become aware of those parts of you that are most beautiful, peaceful, inspiring, wise, and joyful.

Talk to your child as you go about the day. Tell them what you do in your work, tell them about the activities you will do together after they are born, and tell them what you like most in the world they are entering. Tell them about the people you love and the people who inspire you. Share with them the beautiful music you love, and the most peaceful and encouraging words from books or poetry. Take a walk in a place you enjoy, and pray together as you walk.

When you are alone, speak out loud to your child. Tell them your innermost thoughts, your dreams for the future of the earth, your vision of God, or of heaven. Or sing songs that express your highest love for life, your love for your child, or your love for God or the spirit of creation. Use whatever words make sense to you; your baby is listening to the energy and emotions brought up by your words.

Make promises to your child—promise to love them with your most joyful love. Husbands and wives make vows to each other, so why not parents to their children? The relationship between mother and child is much deeper than marriage—you can never get divorced! You are your child's creator, so speak loving words to your creation, and you will give them immense joy.

Remember, our only real purpose on this planet is to feel joy and share it with others. If you adopt this mindset while pregnant, your child will be born with this mindset already in place. This is the greatest education, and the highest service to God a parent could possibly give. Think of the love that Jesus brought to the world, and then imagine what would happen if even 100 of the world's mothers began to love like Mary today!

⚜ Exercise 3: Fathers Share Their Love

Fathers can share their love with the unborn child through the mother. This first practice is good to do once a week when mother and father have quiet time alone together. Choose a time when you can sit peacefully and concentrate on each other. First, take hands and look into each other's eyes. You can speak words of appreciation, or simply look into each other's eyes with love. When you are both relaxed and focused, the mother places the father's hands on her belly and holds her hands on his. Then together send love to your baby. You can greet the child with words, or you can send love silently from your heart through your hands to the baby. Welcome the baby in a loving, joyful spirit, the way you welcome a dear friend at a party you planned especially for them. To conclude, look back into each other's eyes and thank each other for spending this time together.

The next practice is good to do before parents go to sleep. The mother positions herself comfortably, either reclining or laying down, and the father rests his face close to the mother's. Now the father can communicate with the child by speaking very quietly into the mother's ear! The father can tell the child how much he loves the baby on the way, he can sing or hum favorite songs, he can make his promises to the child, he can ask the child questions, tell stories, tell the child about his life thus far, and so on. This should be done very softly and peacefully. What is said is not so important—what is very important is the careful attention given to the baby. Also important is the practice for the father to express his deepest love. The mother can even fall asleep while the father is talking, the child will still get the message, and this is a wonderful way to fall asleep.

✎ Exercise 4: Communicate in the Language of Joy

Hold your child in your arms often. Hold them close, feel the warmth from your heart flowing into their body, and feel the love flowing back from the child into every cell of your body. Very young children naturally let the love they receive flow through them, which is why people feel so good when they hold a baby. The adult is actually feeling their own ability to love, returned immediately back to them by the baby, like a mirror reflecting light.

Look into your child's eyes. Gaze gently into their eyes and send love from your heart to your child. When spending this time together, think only of how beautiful your child is, and how fortunate you both are to have met in this lifetime. Admire each other. Feel proud of your child, feel appreciation for how well your lives are unfolding, feel gratitude for all the wisdom you have to share with each other. If you do not feel much in the beginning, just continue to think on these ideas and you will begin to feel more and more.

You, like Mary, have been chosen out of all the people in the world to care for your child. The universe in its infinite wisdom has place one unique spirit with you, for the particular gifts only you can give. What an honor! This opportunity will never present itself again in all of time, so you must take advantage of it now. Imagine Mary's resolve when she learned how important her child was to the world, imagine her intensity of purpose! You have been given a purpose just as high. Your child has a divine mission within them, a purpose in life that will wither without your love, and thrive with it! Compassion, strength, and vision come from an overabundance of love, love so great that no darkness can overcome it. There is no greater gift you can grant your child, or yourself. A gift of one hundred billion dollars is nothing compared to this.

When you hold your child, feel warmth radiating out from your heart. Whatever has happened outside of that moment, leave behind all those things and feel love when you hold your child—you are holding your creation in your arms! When you spend time with your child, put away all other concerns. Forget your worries and problems, and focus on being together. Give your child your attention, look into their eyes and celebrate your creation!

The idea is to go beyond what most mothers do, to express love to an unusually high level. This is This is the greatest gift you can give your child—a strong personal connection with the woman who created them. We humans cannot live without loving bonds! We may go on breathing, but without love we are like walking computers. And again, providing food and medicine and hugs is not love. You could hire a nurse to provide those things. Your higher mission is to create a deep spiritual relationship with your child. This is done by creating experiences of shared joy.

✒ Exercise 5: Mary Energy for Everyone

You do not have to have a parent-child relationship to practice Mary Energy. Practicing Mary Energy is connecting to your divine ability to love without limits, and there is no one in the world who does not want to feel this love—not one!

Choose an object of love and send love to that object. It does not need to be a husband or wife, boyfriend or girlfriend. You can send love to anyone. Send love to your parent, to your niece or nephew, to any person to whom you feel connected. You can send love to someone you just met. You can send love to a person you have not seen in many years, or to someone who has died. Make a picture in your mind of the person's face, or an image of the joy they inspire you to feel. Then let the love flow out from your heart. Your love can fill up the room where you sit, it can expand to fill the city where you live, and even expand to flow through the entire world. Do this whenever you wish to experience love, whether or not the object of your love is present in your life.

Mary Energy is also not limited to human beings. Practice sending your love to your dog or cat! Many people have the experience of connecting to inner joy when playing with a pet for the same reason that people feel joy with children—animals immediately accept our love, so we feel our love reflected back to us. If you do not have a pet, all the rest of nature also desires your love! The ocean desires your love, and the trees and insects desire your love. Even the spirit of love needs your love.

✄ Exercise 6: Mary Energy Group

The purpose of a Mary Energy group is to learn from your contemporaries how to love more like Mary. Form a small group of people who are interested in practicing Mary Energy and dedicate a time to meet once per month. The participants can be current or future mothers or fathers, or anyone who is interested in increasing their ability to experience and express limitless love. Each participant is both a student and a teacher as the group learns about Mary Energy from life experience.

At your meetings, share some light food and conversation, and then sit together. Light a candle or place a picture of Mary in the middle of the group if you like, as a symbol of quiet focus on the subject of love. Then one member of the group speaks for 10-20 minutes about how they experience Mary Energy. This does not need to be a prepared speech. It is an open reflection on how you experience love, and the effect that experiencing love has on you. The experiences could come from your love relationship with your children, with your spouse, with your life's work, with service to God, or another area. The purpose of this time is to learn from each other, so the other participants should listen attentively and make notes on what is said.

When the speaker has finished, leave five minutes for quiet reflection to meditate on the subject of love. Then gather in a circle and say a short dedication to Mary, for example:

> *"Mother Mary, teach us to love*
> *as you loved your son. Inspire us share your*
> *love more and more each day."*

Between one meeting and the next, each participant reflects on what the other members of the have shared, and on how they can express more love in their lives. Make note of the various ways you experience divine love in your life. Act on any new impulses to love more freely or to feel more joy. Notice any changes that take place in yourself, your environment, and the people you come into contact with in your daily activities. These are insights you can share with your group.

If there are any pregnant women in your group, the group can make a practice of sending love to the mother and her baby. Spend five minutes with each pregnant woman present, focusing on her unborn child and silently sending your highest expression of love to mother and child. Ask Mary for her blessing and her guidance.

After each participant has taken their turn sharing their experience of universal love, devote the final meeting to talking together about what you can learn about love from Mary. Discuss how Mary's love left the universe a better place than before she came into it. Discuss Mary's inspirations to love to such an incredible level, and discuss her joy—it is truly indescribable!

> *"Love is a journey*
> *and a destination of endless joy."*
> Amarjit Singh Modi

❧ Exercise 7: A New Holiday

When a child is born, we greet the new baby, but first we honor the mother! Let's make December 24th "Mary Day." The day before we give thanks for Jesus' birth we give thanks to his mother for giving him to the world. A holiday celebrating Mary not only remembers her contribution, it also celebrates the energy of divine love in our lives. This is not only Jesus' birth, it is the birth of love within you, the renewal of life within us. This holiday is the "day of remembrance of God's gift of love to all creatures."

Pay tribute to Mary and celebrate your gift of love by experiencing joy! Express love with those you love, share the spirit of love with everyone, as you walk on the street, whatever you do! If you wish, start a tradition of a ceremony on December 24th. Gather with a few beings you love, your spouse or your children, or with your pets. Celebrate the high expression of love that was Mary's gift to Jesus. Ask Mary to inspire you to a higher level of love in the coming year. Make a promise to yourself to express your true, joyful nature. Thank Mary for her guidance and ask her to be our teacher. Ask her to bless us so that we may learn to love as she did, make a beautiful gift of our lives to the universe, and celebrate in communion with the energy of boundless love. Every human being on the planet can celebrate this!

FUTURE BOOKS
from Amarjit Singh Modi

Gems from the Cosmos
Timeless Jewels of Universal Wisdom

Feng Shui of the Mind

The Five Finger Path of Happiness

❧ ABOUT THE AUTHORS ❧

AMARJIT SINGH MODI is a world-renowned palmist, psychic, meditation teacher and healer. Born and raised in Kashmir, India, he realized at an early age that his calling was to teach and inspire others. With forty years experience in the spiritual arts, Singh Modi has acquired a vast knowledge of the holy scriptures and writings of all the world's religions. He has read more than fifty thousand palms in one hundred eighty-nine countries. His journey to spiritual enlightenment has taken him all over the globe, and his love of people has made him several hundred friends on each continent. He shares with each one the wisdom he has gained from his life and study, and in doing so empowers people to live life as the adventure it is. One of Mr. Modi's primary tasks in this life is to prepare the planet for the coming messiah. He believes that she will be a woman; a musician from the Middle East, coming to restore peace and harmony to the planet by balancing the male and female energies. He lives in New York City since 1971.

ELIZABETH TEMPLE also lives in New York City. *Mary Energy* is her third book with Mr. Modi.